The Short Cheap Tax Book for Everyone

50 plus things that everyone should know and do, but nobody does

Kirk Taylor

Updated January of 2019

Copyright 2017-2019 Kirk Taylor

To the extent that the book uses specific numbers, they are for the 2018 tax year (returns being filed at the beginning of 2019). I will update periodically, but the book is designed such that you don't need to get a new copy every year (but it's cheap, so do it anyway, that way I know you love me!)

Print a Copy of Your Tax Return

What a stupid first page. I mean seriously, isn't this obvious?

Based on how often I'm asked to get someone a copy of their tax return in the middle of summer, no it's not. Print a copy, put it with all the supporting documents, and throw it in a safe place. I like one of those small, top opening file boxes. I keep stuffing them in until the new one doesn't fit, then I shred the oldest one. You should have 4 years at a minimum, but I probably have 7 to 10 years in there. While you're at it, if you can get an electronic copy, save that on your computer, and your backup hard drive, and maybe even a floppy disk (ask your Dad if you don't know what that is). When you move, these files go with YOU, not in the moving van.

Let me add that, a little time spent anywhere that people ask tax questions (God help me, Reddit is a cesspool of tax ignorance), will enlighten you that needing information from a prior year tax return is the absolute most common tax topic. You can't even e-file your current tax return without knowing your prior year AGI. Most people don't know this because their software remembers it for them and/or a professional doesn't need it. Need to file FASFA, or buy a house – you're gonna need that tax return. And that letter from the IRS…well, you know…

If this chapter looks familiar, it's because I include it in almost all my books, and on my blog, because it's just that important.

Update Your Address with the IRS and Your State

I know these first two chapters are going to make it seem like this book is going to be filled with a bunch of really obvious stuff, BUT, these first two chapters are based on REAL LIFE. At least 25% of all the tax problems I'm asked to help with wouldn't have happened, or would be a lot easier to handle if these first two pieces of advice were followed. So…Update your address with the IRS…

EVERY TIME YOU MOVE!

Believe it or not, the IRS doesn't automatically know that you've moved, and relying on the US Postal Service to forward your mail is not a great idea. The IRS sends letters to the address on your tax return if you haven't formally changed it through them. If the letter suggests a change to your tax return, the clock starts ticking on disputing it as soon as they send it. Updating the IRS when you move will save you a TON of heartache. Failure to do this happens way too often, and the problems it causes are way too easy to prevent. Here's an IRS site with more information: https://www.irs.gov/taxtopics/tc157.html (Link #3)

You're on your own for the state, but their Revenue Department website should make it easy.

Recently I had three clients who were getting ID theft PINs from the IRS and didn't update their address. There is almost no way to fix this and avoid having to paper file.

Don't Fear the IRS

If you're not cheating, you have very little to worry about beyond money and hassle.

Professionals like to scare you with the IRS, and, if you're cheating, you should be scared. I prefer to scare people with the prospect of not getting all they deserve. Let's put it this way: Say you've got a nice desk to donate to charity. You check some stores and eBay, and the values are between $500 and $1000 dollars. Assuming the $1000 isn't a huge outlier (5 sites between $500 and $550 and one at $1000), take the $1000. It's reasonable, defensible, and not frivolous. If you're in the 22% tax bracket, that's $110 on your tax return, plus some from the State. Now let's say the mean old IRS does its worst, and face to face audits you. The auditor looks at your documents and tells you the desk's only worth $500. You argue a bit, but he insists and you have to pay back the $110, plus a bit of interest. No handcuffs, no jail-time, no yelling or beatings. You shake hands, sign some paperwork and write a check. Now let's pretend we're in Vegas. You find a table that gives you $110, and then spins a wheel, and if you lose you have to give them the $110 back, plus $15, except you only lose 1 out of 100 times! Who wouldn't make that bet? That's the same thing we're talking about with the desk. JUST DON'T CHEAT!

Don't Lie to the IRS

Don't ignore them either.

Exaggerate, stretch, manipulate, but don't lie. Two things the IRS hates more than anything, being lied to and being ignored. They're like your Mom.

I encourage taking the most aggressive tax position you can that's not a lie or frivolous. Frivolous is roughly defined as a position that less than one out of three knowledgeable tax pros would consider allowed. That said, if you get aggressive, you need to be prepared to lose in a fight with the IRS. Know how much money you're risking by being aggressive, and be prepared to pay some or all of it back at a later date. Odds are you'll get to keep the money, but it's good to be prepared.

Your Tax Pro Might Not Be A Pro

You can be a paid tax preparer.
Right now.

All you need is a Tax Professional ID Number (PTIN) and you can get that online in 5 minutes for less than $100. No training, no test, nothing.

Don't believe me? Ask the IRS: https://www.irs.gov/tax-professionals/understanding-tax-return-preparer-credentials-and-qualifications (Link #4)

Your tax guy may not even be able to represent you at an audit.

I think you need an Enrolled Agent or a CPA (if they have EA after their name, like, say, Kirk Taylor, EA, then they are an Enrolled Agent – or a liar). If you use a CPA, make sure they specialize in taxes like yours. CPA's know a lot more than Enrolled Agents, just not necessarily about taxes.

Pick your preparer wisely – get referrals. If you don't like what's happening at the desk, don't like the results, or don't like the fees, take your papers and walk out. If the preparer isn't okay with this, and still wants you to pay, then you made the right choice by leaving.

Good preparers don't expect to be paid unless the client is 100% satisfied.

The Tax Prep Guarantee You Get Isn't What You Think It Is

Unless you pay your Tax Dude extra, he probably isn't providing you the kind of guarantee you probably think you deserve.

Most guarantees cover interest and penalties, not taxes. This makes sense, since you would have owed the taxes anyway if the idiot hadn't messed them up. So, by him paying the interest and penalties, you get an interest free loan from Uncle Sam. This is, of course, little consolation when you have to come up with three grand to pay your Uncle back because your Tax Genius turns out to be a Tax Dunce (I personally would only have taxes done by a SUPER Tax Genius).

He (or she) may also charge you for help in responding to the IRS, especially if you get a face to face audit. Also, many will try to claim that you didn't provide them the right information and documents (and they will often be right).

Oh, and that guarantee you get with your software – it's not worth squat.

Get Your Kid's W-2

I tell my clients with kids to tell them: "As long as you live at home, your W-2 comes directly to me."

Kids have a tendency to have their friend's Mom file their taxes for them and, usually inadvertently, claim themselves. Most times it doesn't even change their refund amount!

What it does do, is prevent the parent from electronically filing, which is a major delay. Now, I usually offer to do the kid's cheap or free, and this allows the parent to pretend that they're doing the kid a favor. It also helps me to get the kid dependent on my services, so he can pay me a lot of money when he gets a real life! The actual reasons are more complicated - mainly that it allows me to be sure the parents meet all of the required rules to claim their working child since some of the little bastards like to make REAL money and screw up the dependency tests - ingrates.

Get a Professional Tax Review Once in a While

Tax software sucks.
It really does.

It's designed to be user friendly and easy to use. This does not result in accuracy. Odds are good that a skilled professional will find errors, and maybe more money for you. That doesn't mean you have to pay for the review. Most pros will check your return for free, and then quote you a non-obligatory price for them to fix it. his is a win-win.

Do this every three years at least. You get peace of mind, and maybe some money.

This doesn't just apply to software. If you have been using the same tax pro for years, without really paying attention to the results, you might be getting screwed. Give a new guy (or gal) a chance to see what they can do.

This, of course, does not apply to me – I am perfect – akin to the Tax Unicorn.

Tax Resolution Companies Are Often Rip-offs

You know the ones I'm talking about. The ones advertised on TV or radio that say they can reduce your back taxes by thousands, get the IRS off your back, stop the garnishments, etc.

I'm sure some might be good, legitimate companies, but most are little more than one trick ponies. They'll file an Offer in Compromise (OIC), which will stop the liens and levies (as they promised). Unfortunately, the IRS doesn't approve many OIC's so, when they say no, the problem comes back full force, and you're out a bunch of money you paid to the tax resolution company. If you owe back taxes, talk to a local professional with good references.

As a general rule, an OIC requires doubt as to whether you owe the taxes assessed, or a doubt that you will EVER have the ability to pay it back. This is a long, slow, uphill battle with a high likelihood of failure, and the resolution company will make you do most of the work you thought you were paying for.

Head of Household Doesn't Mean What You Think It Does

Well it might, but it certainly doesn't mean what it says.

Head of Household essentially means Single Parent. You have to have a kid (or other qualifying dependent) who lives with you at least half the year (unless they are a parent) and you have to pay at least half the cost of the place you and them live. You also can't be married as of 12/31 of the tax year, though there is an exception if you didn't spend even one night with your spouse in the last half of the year.

There are a lot of complications to this, but if you live alone and don't support a relative, you probably aren't Head of Household filing status, even if you're the Head of your Household.

If you are a single parent, unmarried, living with and supporting your own child, you are probably Head of Household.

Child Support and Alimony normally have no effect on this situation. If you are the non-custodial parent, you aren't Head of Household no matter how much Child Support you pay unless a different qualifying person lives with you.

If your situation is not obvious, check with a pro.

Don't Do It Just for The Tax Benefit

There are very few things that will improve your taxes without costing you in life.

You only get a portion of that deduction off your taxes, so often times not paying something is better than getting the deduction. People who tell you not to pay off your home mortgage because it's your best tax deduction are just stupid. You pay $10,000 in interest to get $2200 back on your taxes, assuming the 22% tax bracket. BRILLIANT! You're out $7800.

Now the tax benefit combined with other realities, like you don't have $200,000 to pay the mortgage off or you have better things to do with the money can make this a smart idea, but don't just do it for the taxes. I will cover some cool things to do to save on taxes that don't hurt in real life, and cover some that hurt a little, but then I'll tell you how to make the decision the best way possible.

That's why you bought the book, right?

Prepare for Kidaggedon

Assuming that your 18-year-old is going to remain on your tax return is not a good idea.

Kids are worth less and less on taxes as they get older, unless you are paying for their college. You get a bit of a warning shot when they turn 17 and the $2000 Child Tax Credit turns into $500, but 18 is when it's really dangerous.

Sure, your kid may spend the next 4 or 5 years in school, getting you great deductions and awesome Education Credits, but maybe not. A great job, a marriage, a move in with their snuggle bunny, a going on a Jack Kerouac adventure for 4 years, or even just not going to school and working a job that makes more than a few thousand dollars will ruin this INSTANTLY - maybe with no warning.

I encourage people to start adjusting their withholding the year their kid turns 16. Making adjustments such that when their child is 18, they can be gone from the tax return completely and you still won't owe. Besides the obvious benefit of being prepared for them to drop off the return, this gives you a couple of years to ease into the MASSIVE drop in refund Kidaggedon causes, without the increased withholding ruining your budget. If your kid does the right things and remains on the tax return, you get a nice fat refund. If they drop off, you don't have to write a big check to the IRS.

Quick Kid Age Summary: 13 means no daycare credit, 17 means the $2,000 Child Tax Credit drops to a $500 dependent credit, 18 they control a lot of stuff that can mess you up, 19 they need to be in school to keep things easy, and at 24 they're not claimable in many cases. The child being disabled can adjust many of these numbers, but it's complicated so you will need to ask a professional. NOTHING changes the 17 year old credit drop from $2000 to $500.

A Big Refund Isn't Necessarily Bad

I know what everyone says, "A refund means you gave an interest free loan to the government!"

Technically, they're right, but have you seen interest rates lately?

Their opinion carries weight, and let me tell you when a big refund really would be bad: If you're really struggling to make your monthly bills, barely getting by paycheck to paycheck, but get a big refund, you really should adjust your withholding to cut down the struggles.

Other than that, here are a few reasons it's okay:

1. Interest rates suck. If saving the money for a big purchase is your plan, you really aren't losing much letting the government keep it and getting it on your refund.
2. Most American's (myself included) suck at saving. We tell ourselves that we're going to save money, and we may even open a savings account. And there it is; mocking us, tempting us until we spend it! Or even more often, we delay opening the account up because we "need" the money "just this once" and next thing you know, we've saved diddly!
3. Getting a big refund is a good way of ensuring you can catch up if you have a bad year with bills. You get a little behind because, as most American's, we're not really great at budgeting. The credit cards build up a little more than we wanted, and maybe even get a little hard to pay, then BAM! It's refund time and we can do a reset. Now I'm not recommending this as a planning method, but I see a lot of reality in the tax office, and this is a big helper for a lot of people.
4. It's really difficult getting a small refund without ending up going too far. I can say with absolute certainty that virtually every person I do taxes for would consider a $500 balance due as nearly end of the world bad. It SUCKS owing the government money. Even the ones who want to get a small refund would rather get too big a refund than owe one thin dime! Trying too hard for a small refund risks the evil balance due. If you really want to play around with getting the numbers perfect, the IRS has a Withholding Calculator:

https://www.irs.gov/individuals/irs-withholding-calculator (Link #5)

So relax. Tell the naysayers to mind their own business. If you want a big refund, that's fine with me.

Merge Tax Deductions into a Single Year

A lot of deductions have income limits that make them less effective when taken every year. Examples are Medical Expenses and even Itemized Deductions themselves.

If you have a big one-time Medical Expense that is close to or above 10% of your income, it's time to move up elective medical expenses into that year. Glasses and dental work are great examples. Also, make sure to fill all your prescriptions in December of that year. This assumes you itemize your deductions already. Speaking of which, the IRS gives you a Standard Deduction ($24,000 for a married couple for 2018) so you have to get above it in order to change your tax results. If most years you're just below it, it's best to pick a year every so often, and pack elective deductions into that year, especially charity. I don't usually itemize, so I accumulate stuff in my house over a few years until I'm one bad weekend away from an episode of Hoarders. Then I give it ALL to Goodwill and take a MASSIVE tax deduction, netting myself an AWESOME tax refund, which I then spend on fancy dinners and beer.

There's a Tax Hit for Canceled Debt

If you get someone you owe money to reduce or eliminate the amount you owe, that is a call for the happy dance. That is, until the 1099C comes, which sometimes doesn't happen for a while, or at all - but the IRS gets it. Then a CP2000 letter appears saying you owe money on the canceled debt as if it were income. Bummer.

The point is, if you get debt canceled, including car repossessions and foreclosures, be prepared for the 1099C, and the tax hit. There are ways to avoid paying taxes on canceled debt, the main ones being insolvency and if it was your principal residence, but these are complex, and you should read my blog posts on the subject, or buy my other book.

Here's the blog post:
http://supertaxgenius.blogspot.com/2012/03/i-got-1099c-now-what.html (Link #6)

Your Refund Might Take Longer than You Expect

The IRS won't even talk to you if it hasn't been 21 days.

The IRS issues 90% of tax refunds (so they say) within 21 days. That probably won't be the case going forward, because a new law REQUIRES the IRS to wait until Feb 15th to process tax returns with Earned Income Tax Credit or Additional Child Tax Credit. If you get back more than you pay in, and it's not due to college expenses, the week of February 27th is your best guess. Also, the IRS doesn't even start accepting returns until late January (Jan 29th for 2018 returns). This means the clock doesn't even START until that day.

You also have to get them to accept the return for the clock to start. If you mess up a name, birthday, social security number, employer number from your W-2, last year's Adjusted Gross Income, or any number of other things, the IRS will reject your return, and the clock doesn't start.

There are a lot of other reasons you might have to wait, primarily, Tax ID Theft – which is the reason the IRS has to wait until Feb 15th for those magic returns discussed above, and a lot of States will make you wait longer. Worst case is that YOU are the victim of Tax ID Theft, and your return gets rejected because one has already been filed with your SSN. You will be waiting a long time if this happens.

Bottom line – never count on getting your refund until you have it. When I first started doing taxes, I had clients who wouldn't pay their December rent because they expected to get a Refund Loan before they could be evicted. When they didn't get the loan or the refund was delayed...things got...interesting. Always assume the refund isn't coming until it's in your hands!

Don't Over Complicate your Records

Many people obsess about making sure every receipt is neatly categorized in perfect folder files, envelopes or fancy notebooks with pockets and stuff. They want to make sure that everything's perfectly ready for the IRS if they decide to audit them.

This is all well and good, but it's probably not going to happen and you've wasted your time. If this is how you want to do things, go for it, but make sure this doesn't keep you from writing everything down in an easy to use format.

For businesses, a good notebook or spreadsheet with all the expenses listed beats the hell out of a box of receipts, no matter how well organized. Save yourself some time. In the 1 in 100 chance the IRS wants to audit you, there's plenty of time to match the receipts to your notebook (and the notebook makes the IRS a lot more trusting if you're missing 1 or 2 receipts).

Your time is far better spent growing your business or making it run more efficiently.

Don't Claim Kids That Aren't Yours

I don't mean they have to be YOUR son or daughter for you to claim them, just not to claim children you aren't legally entitled to claim in accordance with IRS regulations. That sentence was more correct but was too long for a chapter title.

For one thing, this is ILLEGAL and for another, it can get your tax person in trouble, which I'm sure is your highest priority in this situation. Kids create situations where the IRS can hold US accountable for not being suspicious enough about your situation. In most cases, we just believe you – but not for kid credits.

Now think about it, if the IRS is serious enough about it to fine ME 510 bucks just for not being nosy enough, what will they do to you if they catch you!

This is a BIG DEAL, and it involves a lot of money that might have to be paid back. Plus, there's at least one other person who probably knows you're cheating on your taxes, that being the child's parent.

Just don't do it – even if the parent gives you permission.

Don't Let Someone Else Claim Your Kids

Like the previous chapter, the title should be: Don't let someone else claim your kids unless they are legally entitled to do so in accordance with the IRS code and it results in a better situation for you or your household and/or you are legally required to let them.

But that was too long.

Don't let someone else claim your kids illegally.

Be careful about letting someone claim your kids when it's legal for them to do so, but you could claim them as well. Believe it or not, this situation does happen.

Trust me on this one.

When you let someone else claim your kid, especially illegally, they probably won't stop when you tell them to stop. There's too much money involved. Plus, you are complicit in a CRIME.

If you can legally allow them to claim the child, understand who has the control (higher right to claim them) and be sure you trust them and that doing this is best for you, your household, and the child. A tax professional can be indispensable in figuring the numbers out. Once someone else knows your child's name, SSN and birthday, there are very few practical things stopping them from claiming them.

Don't Believe What You Hear About Taxes

Unless you hear about it from a competent professional that you trust, it's very likely to be crap information.

Government websites are usually reliable.
Big financial publications (Kiplinger's for example) are pretty good.
Newspapers and broadcast news are terrible.
Blogs (other than mine), Facebook posts, friends, neighbors...all useless.

Competent tax professionals are the only people you should trust for sure.

You can't even trust IRS employees. Believe it or not, if you get an answer from the IRS over the phone, and it's wrong, it's still on you. You need it in writing.

I wrote myself a note to list all the stupid things about taxes I've heard, but there's just no room, and no way to pick a winner.

The Income Tax is Not Illegal

Forget it.

All those people screaming about not filing taxes and getting away with it are full of crap, even though they may get away with it for a while because the IRS sucks at enforcement.

There are tons of examples: 16th amendment not properly ratified, taxes are voluntary, zero returns, wages aren't income...all CRAP.

The IRS will not only dismiss your attempt to argue this BS, but can actually fine you MORE (a lot more – up to $25,000) just for trying. They can also fine your tax guy or lawyer for arguing these things.

These situations have been thoroughly litigated, many all the way to the Supreme Court. The income tax is SETTLED LAW. Don't fall for these things.

The 7th Circuit Court of Appeals put it best: "Like moths to a flame, some people find themselves irresistibly drawn to the tax protester movement's illusory claim that there is no legal requirement to pay federal income tax. And, like moths, these people sometimes get burned." United States v. Sloan, 7th Cir. 1991.

The IRS Didn't Call You

Unless you are currently involved in communications with the IRS that were initiated by you in person or by the IRS via a letter, that person calling claiming to be the "IRS" is full of you know what.

The IRS does NOT initiate communications via phone calls. Scammers trying to steal your money or identity do. I have already had TONS of people (including me) receive these kinds of calls. If you want a little more reassurance, try googling the number the call came from (if the number is hidden it's DEFINETELY a scam). Chances are the google results will be full of people asking about the number, and MANY people identifying it as a scam. If you want more reassurance, call the IRS (though this is pretty much a waste of time during peak filing periods.) These guys are professionals, and they can often sound very convincing, and will even threaten to arrest you. Swear at them and hang up.

UPDATE: They have gotten more sophisticated and are even sending relatively real-looking letters. Always assume someone calling and asking for money or personal information is a scam – tax based or not. Independently look the agency's contact information up online and call direct.

If they ask you to pay with gift cards…it's a scam. How people think the IRS wants i-tunes gift cards is beyond me.

That Letter from the IRS is Probably Wrong

And if it's from a state, it might not only be wrong, it might be complete crap, and the state might even know it.

Budget strapped states have been pulling a lot of stupid crap and pressuring their agents into generating more revenue from tax audits. Some states, including Maine, California and Virginia to my personal knowledge, have sent letters to non-resident military personnel stationed in their state demanding taxes as if they were residents, or to their residents stationed out of state who are exempt from their taxes.

Only outright fraud or incredible incompetence can explain how they could let this happen. Needless to say, many of these personnel had moved and the letters never made it to them.

But I digress.

ALWAYS be absolutely certain that the letter you receive is
1: Not a Scam, and
2: Accurate, before you send a dime to the agency demanding it. It's a lot easier to win an argument over whether you should send THEM money than it is to get them to send it back!

The last chapter in this book is a sample IRS letter you can use when responding to them.

Let's Talk About Tax ID Theft

There are a lot of misconceptions about this, and things are changing fast, but here's some good information.

A Tax ID Thief isn't stealing your refund. He isn't even technically stealing any money from you, just your Name, SSN and birthday. He's stealing from the government (meaning all of us). He does this by literally MAKING UP a W-2. You see, the IRS doesn't actually verify that your W-2 is accurate, or even exists, before sending you your refund. They just make sure that the filer, and any kids, actually exist, along with a few other things. The thief needs your information so the IRS thinks they're a real person. Once they file with your information, you can't e-file that year…PERIOD. Your refund is safe, just delayed and hidden behind a bunch of ID verification.

If your return gets rejected because it says you already filed, go right to irs.gov and follow the instructions. The IRS and Congress are working pretty hard on this – hence the filing delay in 2016, and the permanent filing delay for certain credits we discussed before.

Right now, W-2's have magic codes that will hopefully stop most of this, but it's in a testing phase this year.

What Not to Do When You Get Married

Don't change your withholding allowances to married.

Unless you have kids or something besides marriage has happened, then nothing has really changed in your tax life (numbers wise). Your combined refund or balance due will probably be very similar to your previous single returns. Married on a W-4 pretty much implies that you are the sole breadwinner in the family (the W-4 is a relic of a more sexist age). If you both just change to Married and do nothing else, you are going to be unpleasantly surprised.

If you really want to play around with getting the numbers perfect, the IRS has a Withholding Calculator at: https://www.irs.gov/individuals/irs-withholding-calculator (Link #7)

Also, Married Filing Separately is usually a terrible idea, especially if you get Social Security, have kids, get an Obamacare subsidy, pay student loans, go to college, or many other things. Good software and tax professionals will automatically check to see if you might benefit from Married Filing Separately.

FYI: If you are married 12/31 of the tax year, you're married for the whole year. Single is no longer a Filing Status option – PERIOD.

Pay Your Child Support, Student Loans and Taxes

The IRS can and will take your tax refund to pay these things and more. It's called an offset, and there's very little you can do about it, though if it's your spouse's debt you can try filing an injured spouse claim to get your portion of the refund. They won't do it on your first missed payment, but when these things go into default, they'll come get it. Other unpaid things that will cause this: military bonuses or pay that has to be paid back, social security or disability payments that have to be paid back, military exchange credit cards that aren't paid, and even unpaid State taxes. There are a lot of things they CAN use this for, but don't, so the list can change any day. You can call 1-800-304-3107 to see if they are coming after your refund, though be aware that debts can be added between the time you call and getting your refund. That number includes all debts EXCEPT Federal Tax debts.

States are getting in on the act and collecting medical bills, property taxes, utility bills and all manner of other debts.

One big sign that the reduced refund you got was due to debt is if the refund is not an even dollar amount.

Set Up an IRS Secure Access Account Now

The IRS (and I) are highly recommending that people get IRS Secure Access setup BEFORE they need it.

Right now, you need this to easily get your tax return transcript online and to get a missing ID Theft PIN. I suspect you will need it for more and more things as time passes. The process is complex, and requires a lot of information, but once done you're good. It can also take a lot of time if you don't have certain things like a cell phone in your name. It uses your credit report as one step in verifying your identity. I'm not going to go into all the details, but here's the website for more information:

https://www.irs.gov/individuals/secure-access-how-to-register-for-certain-online-self-help-tools (Link #8)

Read it, click on the "Get Transcript Online" button, and get it setup.

When in Doubt, Donate It

If you have stuff you don't want, and you're not sure if it's worth the trouble of selling, give it to charity.

Make sure to deduct its REAL fair market value, not what Goodwill is selling it for. Clothes and other used items should be valued based on what a for profit thrift store would sell it for. Make a good list of the items, take pictures of it, and get a receipt. If you go to a drop box, you don't need a receipt but you need the drop box location, and the name and address of the organization who owns the drop box. If you have a garage sale, don't give in to the temptation to mark everything down to nothing at the end. Ask a fair price, dicker a little, but don't just give it away. After the sale, while everything left is still on the tables, take pictures of it all, load it in the car, and take it to a charity.

Remember when I said don't do anything just for the tax benefit? This is one of the BIG exceptions to that advice.

Not All Charity Drop Boxes Get You a Deduction

Many charity drop boxes are for profit companies that sell the items and donate a portion to the prominently displayed charity on the box. You don't get a deduction for these. Either donate to the big-name charity boxes (Goodwill, Salvation Army, Toys for Tots) or do some research to make sure. Many drop boxes will have fine print near the bottom telling you that you don't get a deduction.

I once saw a Marine Toys for Tots drop box that explained how to deduct your donation without a receipt, and included all the information you needed right on the box. Those Jarheads are super squared away.

Your Cell Phone is Tax Magic!

Not as a deduction, but as a tool.

Simple things like the ability to text yourself reminders, make notes for your business and using a mileage app are pretty damn good. All the tax preparation tools and refund status apps are pretty great too, but there's an even bigger miracle.

I have spent years telling my clients to get receipts, take pictures, and make detailed lists of items donated to Goodwill type charities. This year I had an epiphany, and it falls in line with a lot of my non-conventional advice. In many cases, having detailed records is a waste of time if the IRS rules don't prevent you from reconstructing them later. Mileage and cash charity contributions are an example where this is a terrible idea, but for Goodwill, it's amazing! Why make a list of items donated, when you are already taking pictures with your cell phone? Take the pictures, put them in a folder by date of donation, and back them up to your computer. At tax time, hand the phone to your tax guy to estimate values. For the love of God don't use online value estimators. Get a receipt when you drop the stuff off or note location and organization of the drop box.

In the unlikely event that you have to substantiate the donations, you have plenty of time to print the pictures, make lists, and verify values.

Get the Daycare's ID Number Up Front

You need the Employer Identification Number or Social Security Number (SSN) for whoever you pay for daycare services in order to get a credit for what you pay.

When you use an organized, business-like daycare service, this is usually not a big deal. When you use Mrs. Whatshername down the street, this can be an issue. Believe it or not, there are daycare providers who don't want to pay taxes on their income. That's why the IRS wants your baby watcher's ID number before you get the credit. This allows them to match the income to the right person or company. Establish right up front that you will be claiming the credit, and get the name, address and ID number (EIN or Social Security Number) BEFORE you pay them anything.

Your Babysitter Might Be a Household Employee

If you pay your babysitter more than $2000 a year or $1000 in a quarter, you might have to withhold taxes from them (and a lot more).

With what babysitters are charging, you can get to this point quick! Generally, if this person is your spouse, child or under 18 anytime during the year, you can duck this. If you think you might get even close to these numbers, talk to a professional because this involves a significant amount of effort and paperwork.

You can also read Publication 926 to learn more:

https://www.irs.gov/pub/irs-pdf/p926.pdf (Link #9)

Extension Misconceptions

It's an extension of time to FILE, not time to PAY.

The extension gets you out of the failure to file penalty, but not the failure to pay penalty. You are expected to pay what you will owe with the extension, which requires at least some attempt at preparing a return.

Wandering into a tax office to file an extension on the last day of tax season with no documents in hand is practically a waste of time. An extension is better than nothing, but take some time in March to get at least SOME of your income information into your tax dude or tax software.

If you KNOW that you are due a refund, you don't need an extension. If you will be filing by October, don't bother with the extension, there is no penalty if the IRS owes YOU money.

You Don't Have to Pay Your Balance Due When You File

Your balance due is payable on April 15th even if you file your taxes earlier.

Don't wait to file just because you think you will owe. Get your taxes done early so that you will know exactly how much you will owe, and you can start finding the money before it is ACTUALLY due.

Some nitpickers might nag me over the April 15th date, since it can change due to holidays, but it's a fine, generic date to use since it doesn't move very far, and everyone will be reminded if it's on a different date.

Don't Touch Your IRA or 401K

Okay, now that I've got your attention, you can touch it, just talk to your tax guy or gal first.

Really.

Your financial advisor is not a tax guy. Your banker is not a tax guy. Your insurance guy is not a tax guy. Talk to a tax guy or gal first!

I won't give you investment advice, don't take tax advice from the wrong guy.

There are a LOT of rules about taking money out of tax advantaged accounts. These accounts include SEP's, SIMPLE's, IRA's 401K's TSP's, 457's, 403b's and more. There are some exceptions that get you out of taxes and penalties, but they are complicated. I'm not even going to go into them in this chapter.

Talk to your tax guy!

I will add that the withholding is not, "paying the taxes already." The withholding is rarely enough. Meeting an exception to the penalty does not prevent taxation, just the penalty. Some exceptions only count for IRA's, but not 401K's. Some count for 401K's, but not IRA's. Only your tax dude can give you the right advice.

Two examples of bad advice:

1. A client recently took $10,000 out of his 401K to purchase a home. His banker told him that was an exception to taxes. WRONG! It's an exception to penalties, not taxes, and, oops, that exception only applies to IRA's, not 401K's. Unhappy client!

2. Another client, age 59, left her job. She was going to use her 401K to buy a house. A big house. Her financial advisor told her to roll it over to an IRA to avoid taxes while looking for a house. She knew she would pay taxes, but thought she could avoid the penalty. Her financial advisor told her she could. WRONG! Having it in an

IRA when buying the house avoids the penalty on the FIRST $10000 ONLY. The other part of nearly $200,000 was fully penalized at 10%. To add insult to injury, because she was older than 55, she could have taken it out of the 401K without penalty, for ANY reason. Once it hit the IRA, she had to wait until 59 and a half, or meet an exception. That's right, even with the bad rollover, 6 months would have saved her THOUSANDS! Unhappy client!

Over Withhold on Early IRA and 401k Withdrawals

This is one of the stupidest things in the entire tax world. When you take a withdrawal from a tax-sheltered account, the default withholding is 10% if there is no penalty and 20% if there is. This is almost never even close to enough! For routine, monthly or annual, non-early withdrawals, this might be okay. For early withdrawals, it sucks. I guarantee you every tax pro has heard the words, "It's okay, they already took the taxes out." while we stare in dismay at a 1099R with Code 1 (early withdrawal) that is about to DESTROY their tax return. For an early withdrawal, you need your tax bracket PLUS 10% just to be close. If it's a big withdrawal, like to buy a house, you need to account for it driving you into a higher bracket. To be safe, I recommend 35% in Federal and whatever your state tax rate is as a minimum start for early withdrawals. That makes a pretty good argument for not doing it in the first place, but follow this advice if you decide to make the withdrawal.

Even better, call your tax guru and tell them what you are thinking and ask them what to withhold.

Invest in Tax Sheltered Accounts

There are very few sure-fire ways to save money on taxes. This is one of them.

I'm talking about 401k's, IRA's, 457's, SIMPLE's, 403b's, SEP's and all the other fancy account types out there. Many of them can be done right through your job, and come right out of your paycheck. I'll let your financial guy (not a banker) help you navigate which one and why, but all of them save you money on taxes, either now or in the future.

Put as much in them as you can afford.

The only specific advice I will give is that if your employer has a match to your contributions, invest enough to get the match before you do any other investing. Free money beats everything.

As a general rule, the younger you are, the more you should focus on Roth type accounts, but you really should talk to a financial advisor and not just your tax person.

When I said earlier not to do something just for the tax benefit, this is the time to ignore that advice. Talk to your financial advisor AND your tax dude to figure out the right TYPE of retirement account to invest in, and what investments to focus on – but invest in them for sure!

Open a Roth IRA for a Weird Reason

This chapter is not about Roth IRA's in detail. It's about one little, underappreciated rule about Roth IRA's. Many of the requirements for avoiding taxes and penalties on Roth IRA withdrawals involve a five-year rule. You have to have a Roth IRA for at least five years in order to take advantage of many exceptions. The weird thing is that the rule isn't based on individual Roth IRA accounts, it's based on the first time YOU opened ANY Roth IRA account. So, when you're starting out investing, throw a little money into a Roth IRA, just to get the clock started. It doesn't have to be much, and, to be honest, it will probably not actually matter in the long run, but, if it does, you'll be happy you did it.

Obviously, this should not be interpreted as investment advice, or an argument as to what IRA is better for you. It's just a little helpful hint that has a small chance of saving you some grief someday.

Social Security Makes Tax Planning Hard

If you have a modest income and also receive Social Security, you can be in a weird situation where income increases are magnified by the fact that they make more of your Social Security taxable.

In effect, your income might go up by $1,000, and your TAXABLE income might end up going up by $1,500. Withholding is going to have a hard time keeping up with this. The way Social Security is made taxable is by a complicated calculation where they take half of your Social Security and add it to your other income, then compare it to a base amount. The base amount is $32,000 filing jointly and $25,000. Watch out though, you generally get really screwed filing Married Filing Separately if you spend even one night with your spouse. If you exceed the base amount, your Social Security starts becoming taxable. The maximum amount that can be taxable is 85%. This means you just have to look at your tax return every year and see how much of your Social Security was taxable. If it's 85%, you can make as much as you want and not affect its taxability (you're already at the max.) If none is taxable, you can see how close you are by doing the calculation discussed above.

If you're thousands below the base amount, you don't have much to worry about. If you're close, or some amount less than 85% is taxable, you need to pay attention to income increases and plan accordingly.

Note that this is completely different than working and receiving Social Security before full retirement age such that your earnings are limited before you have to pay Social Security back. This is not a tax thing and I'm not that smart about it.

Pay Attention to Capital Gains

This might require professional help, but it's also one of the few ways that you might avoid paying taxes on some income FOREVER. This applies to stocks and mutual funds held outside of retirement accounts. Usually, you should only sell investments based on need for income, or when it makes sense due to investment considerations. Occasionally it makes tax and financial sense to sell investments with losses to offset investments with gains. You should work with your tax guy AND your investment guy on that.

But this post is about a trick that works regardless of your investment strategy or situation.

If you're income is below a certain threshold, you can sell investments that are worth more than you paid for them, up until the point that you just hit that threshold with the gain included. Then you can buy them back, and NEVER pay taxes on the gain. I call this the reverse wash sale. Wash sale rules prevent you from selling investments to take a loss, and then buying them back immediately – but it doesn't apply to selling for a gain.

The income limits for 2018 are $38,700 for Single filers, $77,200 for Joint filers, $51,700 for Head of Household filers and $38,600 for people filing Married but Separate.

If you have carried over losses, this also might be a bad idea.

This is complicated and requires professional assistance, but if you have a low-income year, you can save BUCKETS of taxes in the future.

Don't Miss Mileage Deductions

First though, driving to and from work is commuting, and is almost never tax deductible. But if you drive to multiple work locations, or you have a business, mileage is your best deduction. I like using a mileage tracking app like MileIQ (Link #10), but a mileage log works well. Keep it in your car, and keep it updated with EVERY work-related trip. Date, description and miles driven. That's it. Also, record the odometer reading at the beginning and end of the year. Make sure not to miss trips that are business related, but not necessarily specifically for sales or jobs. Meetings, research and supply runs are good examples.

Mileage is also deductible when you are volunteering, getting medical treatment and moving. Though moving only applies if you are active duty military. Sometimes it won't make a difference, but keeping track never hurts. Make sure to track them separately, since the rates and where deducted vary.

As of 2018, employees cannot deduct expenses, including mileage, and moving expenses are only deductible by active duty military members on Permanent Change of Station orders.

Use Home Equity to Finance Purchases

I actually hate this idea.

If you use your home equity to finance a car, you are basically telling the bank they can have your house if you don't make your car payment.

Now guess what.

Starting in 2018, home equity interest is no longer deductible. So this bad idea is no longer allowed.

I'm okay with this.

Watch Out For a 1099MISC Job

Most people are employees. They get paid on a W-2, and their employer handles Social Security, Medicare and Income Tax Withholding. They also match your Social Security and Medicare out of their own pocket, which is 7.65% of your income. Because of this matching, your employer would rather you be an independent contractor paid on a 1099MISC. This makes all taxes YOUR responsibility.

A lot of times, this is the right way. Real estate agents, a lot of construction work and many commission salespeople would be examples.

Sometimes it's shaky, and sometimes it's horsepucky.

You should find out, as soon as you take a job, how you're going to get paid, especially if you're in construction. If you're going to be on a 1099MISC, read my post on the subject, to make sure you do it right. If you think you should be on a W-2, but they put you on a 1099MISC, talk to a professional about filing an SS-8 and other forms to avoid paying both halves of Social Security and Medicare.

Have an Emergency Fund

This isn't really about taxes, except that a big tax bill is an emergency that would make having an emergency fund nice, and a tax refund is often the easiest way to start an emergency fund. Your emergency fund should be 3 to 6 months of living expenses. The cool thing about having one, is that this dude named Murphy, who has a law named after him, keeps track of who does and who doesn't have an emergency fund. Emergencies happen to people without an emergency fund, and generally don't happen to people who are prepared to handle them.

I told myself I need to expand this chapter to emphasize HOW IMPORTANT THIS IS…so…
Have an Emergency Fund.
Have an Emergency Fund.
HAVE AN EMERGENCY FUND!!!!

You should also have a budget, preferably one that has a budget item that puts money into your emergency fund at a rate that would refill it in 36 months or less. If it gets overfunded you can shift the money to something fun, but budgets keep your money under control, help avoid excess debt accumulation and let you plan for the future.

Divorce, Kids and Taxes are Weird

If you're divorced and have kids, things are unique.

First, the IRS doesn't care what your divorce decree says about custody. To them, the custodial parent is the parent the child spent the greatest number of nights with during the year...PERIOD. No judge or divorce decree can change that. You can't agree with your ex-spouse to change that.

The custodial parent ALWAYS gets the daycare credit and Earned Income Credit, and they are the only one who can use the child to file Head of Household. If your divorce decree says the non-custodial parent can claim the child, they only get the Child Tax Credit - NOTHING ELSE! You have to be careful to make sure to get this right in your software or with your tax pro. If you were divorced after 2008, the non-custodial parent needs a Form 8332 signed by the custodial parent to claim those things.

Step kids are the same as biological kids in the eyes of the IRS, and divorce (or death) does not sever the relationship. The IRS gives no special consideration to the biological parent over the step-parent in cases of divorce.

Child support has no effect on taxes, and nor does alimony beginning with 2019 divorces. Before 2019, alimony was taxable to the recipient, and deductible to the payer. The taxability and deductibility of alimony in pre-2019 divorces was not as cut and dried as it sounds, so you might want to have some tax help if this applies to you.

If your ex is behind on child support, you can treat alimony as child support (nontaxable) up to the point that it equals how much child support was due that year. Example: $5,000 child support and $4,000 alimony due in a year; if only $2,000 gets paid, it's all child support. If only $7,000 is paid, $,5000 is child support and $2,000 is alimony. Obviously, this only matters in per-2019 divorces.

To clarify, it's the year the divorce decree or agreement was final that determines the taxability of alimony, NOT the year it is paid. Pre-2019 divorces continue to have alimony taxed to the recipient and deducted by the payer. Post 2019 divorces are tax neutral.

Don't Go Exempt!

Seriously!

This is one of the worst things you can do!

It is also generally illegal unless you meet very specific requirements.

Some workplaces that pay bonuses have people who go exempt on tax withholding just before bonus time, so they get the full amount of the bonus. THIS IS CRAZY! These people will try to convince you of how smart they are, and try to convince you to do it as well. DON'T! Tax time gets ugly when you do this, especially for the people who forget to change it back after they get the bonus. There is much wailing and gnashing of teeth at my tax desk when this happens - and I have NO sympathy.

The reason they withhold so much out of bonuses is that they skew the calculation of what your annual income will be, and can cause your regular wages to be under withheld. You NEED the bonus withholding to keep you safe. If they over withhold you will get the extra money back when you file taxes.

If Your Tax Pro Tells You to Do Something…Do It

It shouldn't make me as happy as it does when my clients take my advice, but it does.

I spend a lot of time coming up with brilliant ideas (hence this book) and great advice, yet a noticeable minority of my clients ignore my wonderful advice. Often to their severe detriment. Obviously, there are levels to this, but when they get really serious, lean over the table, look you in the eyes and gesture emphatically, it's time to pay attention.

One of my greatest skills as a tax pro is not cursing under my breath when I see that my important suggestions were blown off. This accomplishment is just below this year's goal of not asking, "What year?" when getting the birthdate of a new child.

Pay Attention to Your Withholding

You should check every pay stub, every time, and make sure your withholding is consistent.

The amount coming out of your paycheck for taxes should stay the same if your pay stays the same, go up if your pay goes up, and go down if your pay goes down (obvious, I know). If you want to be extra careful, you can track your year to date withholding numbers and make sure it lines up with the prior year. Payroll people sometimes make mistakes, so you need to keep an eye on this, and find out why if things change drastically. Don't just assume that everything is fine. Tax time is a bad time to find out something's wrong.

A couple years ago, I discovered halfway through tax season that my employer wasn't withholding ANY state taxes. I had to have them withhold ONE THOUSAND DOLLARS every two weeks for the rest of the season to make up the difference.

Call Your Tax Guy When...

You want to take money out of a retirement account.
You want to change your withholding.
You're going to work overseas.
Someone tells you to do something for taxes.
You're selling your rental property.
You're moving money around in nontaxable investment accounts.
You're retiring.
Your income will go up a lot.
You're starting a business.
You are going to be paid on a 1099MISC.
You're retiring.
You get a letter from the IRS.
Anything else that might change your tax situation, or you have any questions at all.

People don't call (or email) their tax person often enough. That's what you pay for. If you use software...email a tax guy you trust.

Don't Call the IRS Unless…

The IRS is under-staffed and over busy. I don't have a lot of sympathy for them, but I do have sympathy for people who really need to talk to them. This means I hate it when people call them for stupid crap that could be handled online or other ways.

Here's a list of when NOT to call them:

1. Your refund is delayed, unless it's been AT LEAST 21 days AND you checked "Where's My Refund" at irs.gov and followed any instructions there (or it tells you to wait).
2. Your tax return has been rejected. If you can't solve it without calling the IRS – mail your return in.
3. You have a non-time sensitive question and it's between January and April.
4. You have a generic tax question. In this case look it up or call a tax pro – the IRS will give you the wrong answer anyway.
5. You need last year's AGI or a copy of a tax return or a transcript (sign up to get them online).

DO call the IRS if:

1. They tell you to.
2. You have a letter with a specific number to call.
3. Your tax pro tells you to.

The IRS Hates MLM Companies (think Avon)

Especially if it's a low effort, low sales multi-level marketing (MLM) business like Avon, Pampered Chef, Party Lights, etc.

The IRS thinks most of them are hobbies, and that most of your expenses are personal and not business. Oftentimes, they're right. Ideally, you need to turn a taxable profit to truly be a business, once every three years gets you the presumption of being a business. If you don't, the IRS will try to reclassify you as a hobby, and your income is suddenly ALL taxable, and, starting in 2018, you get NO deductions! Businesses take expenses right off the top of income before it becomes taxable, hobbies don't.

My advice in these situations is to charge hard for three years, busting your ass to make money, and then, if you haven't, reassess the future of the business, taking into consider your life goals, and how successful you've been.

If you own one of these businesses, I have the book for you:

The Short Cheap Tax Book for Multi-Level Marketing (Link #11)

You're Doing Your Tips Wrong

No one does tips right.

Tax pros HATE tips.

You should be keeping a record of ALL tips, both cash and credit, and reporting them to your employer every week. Your employer should be withholding taxes from your paycheck to cover those tips, and matching 7.65% out of their own pocket as Social Security and Medicare taxes.

This explains why employers are so cavalier about this - less tips reported by you, less matching by them. I can't tell you what to do when rocking the boat could piss off your fellow employees, or make your boss wonder why you were hired in the first place, but I can tell you what the right thing to do is...

…and I just did.

You Can Deduct Sales Tax Paid

If you live in a state with no income tax, you can deduct sales taxes you pay.

This assumes you itemize, which is a lot less likely after the new tax law passed. You can track every bit of sales tax you pay, and save every receipt, or you can estimate based on income, state and family size. The IRS has tables for that. If you use the tables, make sure to include any nontaxable income you have, like military allowances, inheritances or nontaxable disability. You can also add in the actual sales tax for large items like boats and cars.

I tried adding my receipts one year, and it was slightly higher than the estimate, but TOTALLY not worth the effort.

Pay Attention to State Taxes

Your tax software is probably not nearly as good at doing State taxes as it is at doing Federal (and it's not that good at Federal anyway).

Your tax guy might not be that good at states that he doesn't work in either.

It can be very worthwhile to spend some time researching tax deductions and credits for your state, and reading the instruction booklet when doing your taxes. Also, if you have a state tax return done by a professional that's not in that state, ask him about his knowledge of the state, and check things carefully.

In addition, if you work in a state, even if you're not a resident, you probably owe them taxes. Employers can really suck at accounting for this on your W-2. Normally if you live and work in different states, the state you live in taxes everything, the state you work in taxes the income earned in their state, and the state you live in gives you a credit for the taxes you paid to the other state so you're not double taxed. Some states have agreements with their bordering states that modify this. These are called reciprocal agreements and can be very complicated.

Report Stock Sales!

Even when they're small.
Even when you lose money.

This applies to mutual funds as well. Your broker will send you a 1099B or some combination of 1099's that includes the 1099B, if you sell anything during the year that needs to be reported. It will come late, but you should know it's coming and wait for it. The broker will also send a copy to the IRS, and, if you don't include it, the IRS will calculate your taxes as if you paid ZERO for the investment. This means the proposed tax bill can be heart stopping!

If you file your taxes, and then get the 1099B, file an amendment to prevent getting the scary letter.

Don't Trust Your 1098-T

Theoretically, these should be getting better, but they have been awful in the past.

You can get an account transcript from your school, showing what was billed and how it was paid. I highly recommend getting one and using it, vice the 1098-T.

I have a good chapter on education expenses in my other book, but here's the short version:

Ignore student loans, and simply take what was billed for tuition, plus course required books and fees, and subtract money from scholarships, VA benefits or other financial aid that you don't have to pay back. It doesn't matter if you made up the shortfall with student loans, credit cards or cash - those were your expenses. Some credits don't let you include anything other than tuition, so make sure you know which one you're using...

Alright, I'll give more detail...American Opportunity Credit (AOC) lets you use books and fees, Lifetime Learning Credit (LLC) does not. But you really should buy my other book if you have education expenses...it's way too complicated for this book.

AOC is generally for the first four years of undergraduate school and LLC is for pretty much everything else. If you get AOC, definitely print account transcripts and save receipts for books and fees. Your preparer is required to keep copies of these, and the IRS is taking a HARD look at these. In fact, I would say AOC is more likely than anything else to get the IRS's attention on your return (short of leaving income off your return).

If scholarships and grants exceed your tuition, you used tax advantaged accounts such as 529 plans or Educational Savings Accounts, or you used savings bond money for your education, you should seek professional help in ensuring you get this right.

If you get GI Bill or Tuition Assistance from the military or VA, you very likely have almost no education expenses to get a credit for, even if your 1098-T says you do. The IRS is figuring this out – BEWARE!

July 2nd is an Important Date

This is the halfway point of the year.

Actually, it's the last day of the first half for normal years and the exact middle for leap years.

This matters in many situations in which the IRS requires something to be for "at least half the year". If your last kid moves out July 1st, you lose the ability to claim them and you lose Head of Household. So, keep them around a couple more days - and make sure they know you will be claiming them unless they are old or make a lot of money. Some things, like "unmarried for tax purposes" use "the last 6 months" instead of half the year. The point is, if it's June, and a household shakeup is coming, paying attention to what the rules are and how close July is getting can make a major difference on your taxes.

While we're talking about dates, if you're married on 12/31, you're married for the whole tax year, so be aware that Married Filing Separate (MFS) almost always sucks. Good tax pros have mastered the art of not heaving a huge sigh when clients ask them to check the results if they filed MFS.

Download a Copy of the Federal and State Instruction Books

They're free.

Put them on the back of the toilet and read them while you poop.

You would be amazed what you find that might apply to you that your software forgets to mention. Remember, easy isn't accurate, and software tries hard to be easy. You might even find some deductions your tax guy missed! If you do, your tax guy should give you your money back and do the amendment for free - I would.

Have the books handy if you use software to file your taxes or download a fresh copy if you're a germaphobe.

These books also make quite powerful sleep aids - and they are definitely NOT habit forming.

The Kids Get the House When You Die

So that was a clickbait headline because I couldn't come up with a better title that covered everything I want to say.

As a general rule, you want the name on the deed to a house to be the person who owns it and lives there (investment or rental property excluded). The owner occupant has so many tax advantages in so many situations that doing anything else requires very careful consideration.

Giving your house to your children before you pass means that their basis in the house, which is the number used to calculate gains when sold or to determine depreciation when converted to rental or business property is YOUR basis. What YOU paid for it sooooo loooong ago. This can really mess them up when they sell.

I'm really not saying you have to be on the deed no matter what, just talk to tax pros AND estate planners before you do anything else.

Tax Software Sucks

Why does tax software suck? Simple: it has to be both user friendly, easy to use, and accurate. If it's not user friendly and easy to use, no one's going to pay for it. Hell, that's why it's so popular!

It is simply not possible to cover all the complexities of tax law and still be easy to use. So, they make it easy to use: "How much did you pay for uniforms?" Sure, there's an info button you can click that will go into all the nitty gritty of this question, but if you read them every time they come up, it's not simple and easy anymore. "How many miles did you drive for business last year?" Again, many pop-ups will be available to help you navigate the dizzying rules that are involved in this simple question, but you're not likely to read them, and, if you do, they're only going to make you more confused. Don't even get me started on depreciation, business use of home, or investing income!

And that's just the Federal return!

Many states have nearly incomprehensible tax laws, and dozens of deductions and credits that you pretty much need to know exist in order to take advantage of them. Most software just drags things from the Federal to the State, with barely a peep about what deductions you might miss.

I cannot even begin to describe the messes I've seen from tax software! Just recently, a client with one W-2, no wife, no kids, no house, and an amazingly simple Federal 1040EZ missed out on over $10,000 in state tax money over the last dozen years because either the software didn't ask, or he neglected to answer enough questions to establish that his military income was exempt from California taxes. Most of that money is gone forever.

Tax preparation software SUCKS! You will have a better chance at an accurate return using pen and paper with the Federal and State instructions than you will using software!

You Can't Work Overseas for a Year and Pay No Taxes

You actually can, but it's a lot harder and more complicated than those companies that hire people for 1-year overseas contracts make it out to be.

If you sign a one-year contract, and you intend to return after the year, you are on shaky ground. If you leave behind a wife, kids and/or a home, you're in a sinkhole.

The idea is that there's a Foreign Earned Income Exclusion, and, if you establish a tax home in a foreign country, you can exclude over $100,000 of foreign earned income from taxes. The problem is that "tax home" requires stronger ties to the foreign country than to the good old US of A. That's a high bar to get over, particularly for just a year, and even more so if you live on a base or in company housing - and that's just the first of the many pitfalls that are waiting.

There are ways to make this work but I have two critical pieces of advice:

1. Talk to a professional tax dude
2. Withhold as if everything was going to be taxable or save enough money to cover the taxes if withholding isn't available.

There are WAAAAAAAY too many rules to this to just wing it.

What About the Trump Tax Plan?

I covered a lot of this information as it applied to the various chapters, but this is a fairly comprehensive list of what changed. There's not a ton of detail in this section, but it gives you an idea what has changed so you know what sections you need to go back and review. For a lot more detail, <u>The Short Cheap Tax Book for the Trump/GOP Tax Law</u> (Link #12) is available now.

Here is a summary of the tax changes in the final bill that was passed. Unless otherwise noted, they apply to 2018 taxes:

Tax tables are generally better, and the tax brackets went from 10, 15, 25, 28, 33, 35, and 39.6 percent to 10, 12, 22, 24, 32, 35, and 37 percent.

Standard deductions were changed to $12,000 for Single and MFS, $18,000 for Head of Household (HH) and $24,000 for Married Filing Jointly (MFJ) and Qualifying Widower (QW). This sounds awesome, but they eliminated the personal exemption of $4050 for everyone on the return. For kids, this was offset by doubling the Child Tax Credit (discussed below). Effectively, your standard deduction plus exemptions for Single/MFS went from about $10,500 to $12,000. For MFJ it went from about $21,000 to $24,000 and for HH it went from about $13,500 to $18,000.

Claiming Head of Household has been subjected to preparer due diligence rules, so be prepared for more scrutiny from your tax guy and the IRS (starting in 2019 with 2018 tax returns).

The Child Tax Credit went from $1000 to $2000, with up to $1400 refundable. Other dependents who are not qualifying children age 16 and below gets you $500. The income numbers where the credit phased out were dramatically increased to $200,000 for Single and $400,000 for MFJ. This is up from $110,000 for MFJ. If you were in the 25% tax bracket, you almost break even with these changes and the elimination of the exemption. In the lower brackets, you come out well ahead.

You can deduct no more than $10,000 of state and local income and property taxes on your tax return.

NEW home loans in 2018 and later can deduct interest on up to $750,000 of loans, which is down from 1,000,000. Home equity debt interest is no longer deductible. This applies to new loans only.

ALL miscellaneous itemized deductions subject to the 2% of income limitation are eliminated: tax prep fees, employee business expense, investment expense and a TON more.

Casualty and theft losses are only deductible for President declared disasters. There is also a special provision for losses due to disasters that occurred in 2016.

You can deduct up to 60% of your income in "normal" charitable contributions. This is up from 50%. Some contributions have more restrictive limits such as stock that's worth more than when you bought it.

For 2017 and 2018 ONLY, you can deduct medical expenses that exceed 7.5% of your Adjusted Gross Income. Obamacare was phasing in a 10% threshold which will now apply to everyone in 2019 and later years.

The high-income phaseout of itemized deductions was repealed.

The Kiddie Tax was simplified dramatically. Kiddie tax occurs when your child has more than $2000ish of investment income. Children subject to the Kiddie Tax pay taxes at the rate of Estates and Trusts which is higher than they normally would.

You can use up to $10,000 of 529 college savings plan money, per child, per year, on elementary and secondary school tuition and other expenses without paying tax on it.

Moving expenses are no longer deductible and employer reimbursement for moving expenses is taxable except for military Permanent Change of Station moves.

Starting in **2019**, any NEW divorce agreements will have alimony non-taxable to the recipient and non-deductible by the payer.

Starting in **2019**, there is no penalty for not having health insurance.

The Alternative Minimum Tax exemption and income at which it phases out were significantly increased and indexed for inflation.

Student loans cancelled due to death or total and permanent disability are no longer included as income.

Entertainment expenses are no longer deductible. Essentially, anything that is FUN is not deductible anymore. Meals are still 50% deductible for most client meetings.

Most businesses can deduct 20% of their profit off of their taxable income.

Many of the above provisions have expiration dates in the next few years, but if history is any guide, the vast majority will be extended nearly indefinitely.

The following things were NOT changed:

Capital Gains rates are unchanged.

No change to education credits, student loan interest deductibility, or plug-in vehicle credits.

Savings bond interest used for education is still not taxable.

Education provided by colleges to their employees is still tax-free in the same way as it was before.

The exclusion of employer-provided education assistance is unchanged.

Educators can still deduct $250 of in-class supplies they provide in the same manner as before, but anything above this amount that used to be deductible was eliminated with the elimination of the 2% floor itemized deductions.

No change to the exclusion of gain from the sale of personal residence. To be clear - you DO NOT have to buy a new home within 2 years to exclude it, that law was changed 20 years ago.

No change to MSA deductions or employer-provided Dependent Care Benefits rules.

No change to adoption credit or exclusion of employer-provided assistance.

No change to the solar credit. It still starts phasing out in 2020.

There is No 1040EZ or 1040A Anymore

Just the Form 1040.

In an effort to deliver on the promise of a simplified tax form that could be filed as a postcard (not that you ever would, of course) the Form 1040 was modified to put all of the most common items on one half page form, and move all the rest of the stuff to six schedules.

So now, the base 1040 is the only form, and you use schedules as necessary.

To be clear, nothing is simpler than it was before, just moved around.

A Sample IRS Response Letter

This was an appendix in Everyday Taxes, but I think it's useful to include here. I use the same basic style of letter for all of my IRS responses. It's not based on anything required, or suggested by anyone in authority, it has just worked for me and I've had decent success. It's designed to be respectful, to the point and easy to follow and respond to. It's not complicated and should not be difficult to compose. Don't over think it! Be honest! Be Nice!

Here's the format:

Today's Date

To: Internal Revenue Service
From: Your Name, followed by your Social Security Number

Subj: IRS Letter (put the type and any control numbers here - you can find them in the upper right corner of the letter) dated (date on the letter)

1. I received your letter referenced above.
2. Start by telling them any pertinent background, like you didn't get the form referenced
3. Or you forgot to include something
4. Each number should have one, specific piece of information.
5. Acknowledge information they provide that is correct.
6. Then identify where you think they are wrong, but don't be rude.
7. Once you've identified accurate and inaccurate information above.
8. Give them your bottom line belief as to what you feel the result should be.
9. If you don't owe them anything, and they don't owe you....
10. Say, "Based on the above, I don't believe I owe any additional taxes."
11. If you owe a smaller amount, tell them the amount.
12. Ideally tell them you are sending the money, if not, tell them how much you are sending, and how you plan to pay the rest.

13. Tell them what forms and documentation you are enclosing.
14. Thank them for their attention, and/or, if you made a mistake, apologize for the trouble.
15. Tell them to feel free to contact you, and include a method of contact with the information needed to reach you.

        Very respectfully,

        Your Signature

        Your Printed Name

www.ingramcontent.com/pod-product-compliance
Lightning Source LLC
Chambersburg PA
CBHW061202180526
45170CB00002B/925